WELCOME TO
i SPY
4TH OF JULY

THIS BOOK BELONGS TO:

I spy with my little eye something starting with ...

A is for America

I spy with my little eye something starting with ...

B is for Bell

I spy with my little eye something starting with ...

C is for Cake

I spy with my little eye something starting with ...

D is for Decoration

I spy with my little eye something starting with ...

E *is for eagle*

I spy with my little eye something starting with ...

F is for Four

I spy with my little eye something starting with ...

G is for Gnome

I spy with my little eye something starting with ...

H is for Hat

I spy with my little eye something starting with ...

i is for Ice Cream

I spy with my little eye something starting with ...

J is for Jelly

I spy with my little eye something starting with ...

K is for Kid

I spy with my little eye something starting with ...

L is for Love Gnome

I spy with my little eye something starting with ...

M is for Mount Rushmore

I spy with my little eye something starting with ...

N is for News

I spy with my little eye something starting with ...

O is for Owl

I spy with my little eye something starting with ...

P is for pie

I spy with my little eye something starting with ...

Q is for Queen

I spy with my little eye something starting with ...

R is for Rocket

I spy with my little eye something starting with ...

S is for Statue of liberty

I spy with my little eye something starting with ...

T is for Teddy bear

I spy with my little eye something starting with ...

U is for USA

I spy with my little eye something starting with ...

V is for Vote

I spy with my little eye something starting with ...

W is for White House

I spy with my little eye something starting with ...

X is for Xylophone

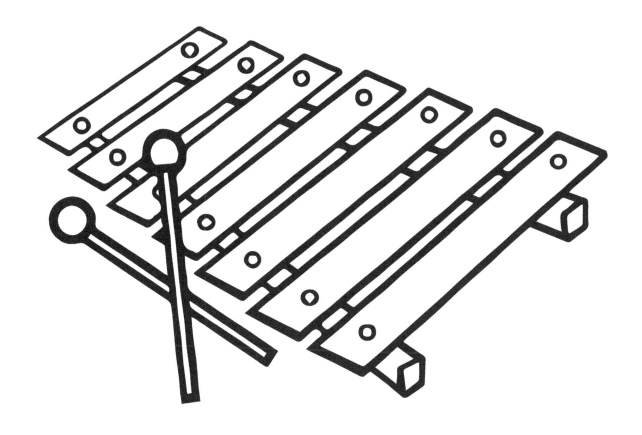

I spy with my little eye something beggining with

Y is for Yarn

I spy with my little eye something starting with ...

Z is for Zebra

Made in the USA
Monee, IL
30 June 2023